HEAVEN

Guiding Poetry to a
Higher Consciousness

You are so worthy.

Look,

not only up, for heaven,
but down
at your hands
and feet;

And know
this is God,

lost in its own beauty.

Chapter 1: Divinity

Fear Set Aside/ to exist
Set fear aside
for what we are about to discover.

Truth.

The answer.

Life.

To live.
To love.

To exist.

At The Gates
This is not a poem.

Show yourself
and truth be known.

Set aside your mask.

Enter the gates;

Or take no steps forward.

Remove the veil;

And take a step; Toward
Heaven.

Blowing Horn
The time has come.

The battle is won.

War is over
and Heaven has begun.

Sound the horns.

We are coming in.

Angels
Hiding in our own creation.

The angel falls
and forgets.

Soon to be picked up
by hands, mighty.

Re-realizing themselves
as one.

Lost in heaven
all along.

Wings/ boundless
Helpless,
yet to bloom.

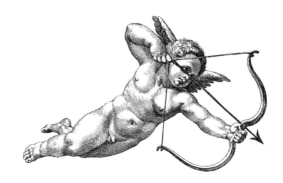

"Human" in
evolution.

We are still in transition.

Boundless.
Awaiting flight.

Unaware of the wings on their backs;
and the freedom

right before your eyes.

Prison of Freedom
Crying.

Calling

Screaming existence.

Expressing in pain.

Passionate,
speaking loud to all and none.

Thrashing.

Raging
in the prison of freedom.

Battle
Beaten,
in the never ending fight of consciousness.

Battling the mind of an angel.

Evil
and god.

Exhausted.

Forcing itself
into a long awaited slumber.

Torture/ecstasy
I have traveled
through the eternal cosmos.

Tortured.

Broke and burned.

Through untold pain.

Hell and back.

Restless;

To bring heaven.

I Am Laughing At You/ laughing with you
I am laughing *at* you;

With you,
through the painful lessons.

Giggling at your head scratching.

Clueless of your beauty.

Oblivious to the truth;
Unaware there is one.

Over and over,
burning your hand.

Reaching for heaven.

Sleeping Angel
You slept through the pain.

Wake up,
rise in heaven.

Wake up,
wake up.

The war

is over.

God Sleeps/ unaware being/ ignorant "human"
God sleeps through stubbornness.

Through anger
and fear.

Rises in the decision to love.

To accept.

Awakens
mighty;

And in control.

Realizing mind.

All the answers
found
in the physics of being.

Wings Ripped Away/ forgotten how to fly
Flight.

Removed
by belief.

By those hurting.

Wingless and still searching.

Beat up.

Teased.

Ripped from your back;

Precious wings.

No remembrance of her beauty

and soaring.

Crying Angel/ falling to earth
Calling me back with pouring eyes;

Never wanting to let go;

The angel cries
stepping foot out of heaven.

Aching.

Pained,
having returned to earth.

Lost but Found
Round and round.

She is lost,
but found.

Existence does not come to an end.

Finding herself in beauty again.

Patched and Sewn/ repaired wings/ you are still an angel
Fly.

Up,
up.

You are beautiful.

You can do anything.

Patched and sewn;

Good as new.

Wings repaired;

And they suit you.

Stepping into Consciousness
Angels surround me;

With music, pain,
and expression.

With laughter and
shrieks.

Suffering;

You have fallen.

I hear you.

See, and feel you.

Caring and crying.

Calling out
to be saved.

Steps to Heaven
From here, I see everything.

Intentions wrong
and true.

Every heart and
regret.

Every fearful moment met.

Desire and dream set.

Higher,
higher,

I see more.

And all you have
yet in store.

Flight/ above the clouds
Looking down,
I see such pain.

Uncertainty,
but beauty in all the fallen.

Earths
scattered angels,
like ants on a hill.

Panic,
without reason.

Each problems so small;

Only a speck of the great all.

Consuming.

Misery.

Waiting to become conscious.

I see selfishness.

And a *gorgeous* blooming.

Conscious Light/ unconscious light
Standing in light of angels.

I know the answers still
to come and correct;

And am conscious of the mistakes.

Choices you will make.

But let the angels rest
and play.

Aloud,
their wishes granted.

Whatever they say.

Still lessons to learn.

Consequences to pay.

Star of the World
You are the star in all the books
of the greatest story ever told.

The fallen
and savior.

The all.

Diseased and reborn.

Courageous and faithful
in every way.

The unfailing hero lives on.

Choir/ orchestra/ chorus
Wailing
voiced opinion.

In
and out of tune.

All that is said comes true.

Dancing to our own rhythm.

Billions of perceptions are
clashing chords.

And with practice,
a choir.

A chorus of angels.

Shining light across the stage
for the greatest performance ever made.

In hopes and prayers
demanding the rid of pain.

Shouting "freedom"
projecting truth

and dreams.

Poets
Poets
penetrate the mind.

Expressing perfection
upon the planet.

Heaven is what exists.

All art,
all things,
perfect.

Without need to interfere.

Knowing poetry is silence.

And the world
only beauty,

and a song to be heard.

Creators of Heaven
Together,
pointing beauty to those
who will follow.

For the infininth time,
falling in love
with the universe;

And each builder.

Inspired;

They see themselves
angels and artists.

And the creators of Heaven.

Step into God
Take your place
upon the throne

Step into God.

Set your arms
upon the rest.

Lay back.

For all is yours.

Your kingdom.

God's Arms
I am held,
reassured and protected.

Wrapped.

Cared for.

Absolutely in love.

Glowing,
in the warmth of God.

God Smiles
There is joy
in the corner of your eyes.

A smile will enlighten them.

And I see you know;

Life will be perfect.

The way it was meant.

Renewal of Earth
In my mind, the world has caught flame.

Burnt to a crisp by the mind
who imagines.

And the ashes will fall to earth.

Fertilized.

Growing back,
fresh and new.

In the burning fire that is truth.

Library
We are awake.

Writers;
And a thousand books
sit high upon our shelves.

Re reading what has been wrote.

And we find ourselves.

Deeply realizing
they are me.

Absolute Harmony/ the great infinity

Earth,
body.

Mind.

Universal harmony
to be known.

Slowly,
reaching the divinity of consciousness.

To see;

The Great Infinity.

Welcome to Heaven

Everything you do;
Good or bad.

All that is decided,
and all that is done.

Accepted and forgiven.

And I welcome you.

Halo
Those who see;

The torus.

The golden ring.

Your halo is earned;

Communicating...

The Universe.

Chapter 2: Truth

Born in Heaven
Along the way,
it is forgotten;

By those speaking.

By all hurting.

Unknowingly projecting;

Washed from purity.

Misconception
of the word.

Muddy,
distracted and unclear.

Too certain of the lore.

Convinced,
generation by generation
that Heaven is earned.

Blindfolded/ trust reality
Just this once,
let go.

Starting now,
test the waters.

A new direction.

Walk blindfolded,
knowing the universe will guide.

Trusting in reality.

Alignment/ enlightenment
Beauty within;

And without.

Lining up with the universe.

Acceptance of self.

Others,
and all that is.

Perfect alignment.

Angel,
be enlightened.

The Universe Imagines/ the creator
Create.

Build.

The universe imagines itself.

Its creations.

Its reality.

The Thinker/ not what it seems
Let go
of what you think you know.

Release beliefs
to see the fantastic,

horrific reality.

You are the creator;

The name giver.

The artist,
and thinker.

Imagining.

Creating.

Held in state of dreaming.

This is not what it seems.

Eternal Life/ eternal waking

It does not allow
itself conscious
of such horror.

Forever,
life is lived.

As life is all there is.

Napping through the pain.

Without wealth.
Without love of itself.

Sleeping through unconscious
decisions made.

Rising, in time of health,
communication.

Technology.

Preservation
and peace.

And *it*
is only waking.

Only Dreaming/ greet me with poetry
This is only imagination.

A dream.

And when the fire reaches us,
know that pain is only temporary.

Burning away.

Scream
our last breath.

A horrific,
romantic death.

And be awakened
in a world with only you and me.

Greeted with poetry in the morning.

Shaking You Awake
Still dreaming.

Resting until ready to wake.

Sleep in perfection.

Sleep through your creation.

I will wake you
when you're ready.

Shake you
with the magic
of poetry.

Dreaming of Separation
It is only a dream
that all is not one.

A nightmare you will wake from.

Frightening,
killing
and stealing.

Lying and dying.

Only misleading
that the world is fighting;

But in a deep
deep sleep.

Dreaming
of separation.

Slow Awakening
I thought this was reality.

No.

Tired.
Only waking.

There is truth
set aside;

Just for me.

What is shared;

Read,
here and now.

This.
Moment by moment.

Another day.
Another dream.

Rubbing your eyes.
Be enlightened.

Slowly awakening
in the sunshine
that is poetry.

Here and Now
This is what exists.

What you see before you.

This thought, itself.

Not any future,
nor any past.

With access to all.

No secrets hidden.

Knowledge of the universe.

Here and now.

Thought/ I am thinking
I am life.

I am existence.

I am thinking.

I am reality.

I am God.

Conscious Voice/ ability to think/ what is?
What you hear is mind.

Fed in your sleep,
demons,
god,
trauma.

Words of existence.

Pre,
and re written.

From all who has lived.

Interpreted.

Those of the wise,
and of ignorance,

Now coming into a listening preference.

What is real?
Which is which?

What is anything?

What is, at all?

Dust/ chemistry/ physical being
Dust of the infinite.

Cosmos
swims throughout your veins.

Creature within creature.

Chemistry of skin and brains.

I am air, and fire.

I am
THE UNIVERSE.

Water that floods
the earth.

Then burns.

The observer.

Heat that lights the sun.

Everything.

Everyone.

Without Name
What have you called this experience of being?

What have you been calling yourself?

Made up,
imagined.

Meaningless.

These, too, are only sounds.

All words called out.

Those
and that around you;

Vibration of your voice.

Carbon dioxide, met in oxygen.

And the name does not exists.

Life
What you have called life.

Existing.
Being.

Feeling.
Hearing.
Tasting.
Smelling.
Seeing.

Thinking.

The conscious universe
interpreting self
and meaning.

In patterns repeating.

The Magic of Existence
That without name.

What *is*.

The all;
Life, and everything in it.

God.

Magic you call,
existence.

Experience of Life

Crows feet
at the corner of my eyes.

My face shows the truth.

Cracked at the edge.

Creases in my skin.

Wrinkles on my forehead.

I am experienced.

Years
of laughter.

Surprised
by reality.

All as One/ infinity/ one universe

All that is,
is God.

All that can,
has and will be.

Existence.
Infinity.

Yourself, God

The reader,
the writer.

All else,
God.

One truth.
One reality.

One being,
one mind,
one universe

All as one.

No You, Nor Me

Separated by language.

Sounds made in the name of reaction
pleasures and pain.

No matter what it is named.

All is the same.

I, This, We
I,
this,
we are god.

This being.

This experience.

This very moment.

This

is God.

Everything.

Existence and reality

The Many Names of God

Universe,
space,
earth,
atom,
self,
DNA,
ether,
all.

Motion, matter.

Magnetism, radiation.

Life,
perception,
presence,
consciousness,
observation,
pain,
expression;

Are the many names
of God.

I Am
God is only a sound.

Noises made,
expressing what is observed
and learned.

Interpreting itself.

Only being.

You
Speak the absolute.
"I am God"

Say out loud,
"I am perfect"

You.

You can do anything.

You
are every single thing
waiting to be understood.

You

You
are God.

You Are That
You are that which observes the universe.

That which examines itself.
That which you call Earth.

That which creates.

That which imagines.

And that which is.

That which gives itself a name.

You are that.

That which builds reality;

That which has ever been.

That which cries,
trying to communicate it exists.

That which learns.

That which hurts.

That what you have called, Heaven.
Born in its dirt.

That which longs to know the truth.

It is you.

You are that.

Future/ past/ eternal now
I know the future
and past.

For us to discover
like clock work.

The creature we call "Human"
or "thought"
is discovering the atom.

Technologies all the same
on a course of existence.

As all intelligence creates the cup.
All the amplifier,
and the radio
And things mobile.

So too, travel the galaxy.

Communication.
Relations.

Each with vehicle, and social law.

We will discover the all.

The time is now,
where we build again.

"Humans" must wake,
or be put to end.

Collection of Experiences/ collected knowledge
All is experiences.

You are a walking bundle of all that is.

Collections of the galaxies
from all that has ever been.

Sadness, heartache
smiles and joy.

Hard work, pay.

Progress and forwardness

Flawless Universe
Do not worry.

Step forward.

Cross the bridge now;
into the arms of the universe.

Caught and picked up.

Never to fall.

Reasons/ why do we live?/ life is.
Cause,
effect.

Tide together throughout existence.

Everything happening for a reason.

Here we are again.

Exactly aligned
for this encounter.

We live
because it is…
existence.

The universe exists.

So life
and consciousness.

Purposeless/ without meaning
Nothing matters.

Life has no purpose, but just is.

As it is only existence

Do all that you wish and will.

As it is only nature.

Let a meaningless existence
set you free.

Live without worry.

Exist comfortably.

Truthfully.

Peacefully.

I Am Pain/ I am desire
I thought I had left desire behind,
so many times,
but it is always the same.

I have smiled infinitely through the pain.

Given eternity to find humour
and romance in it again.

Blown away by the beauty
of being fooled.

A mirror is held up
and its eyes sparkled.

I am pain and desire.

Still, I wish for eyes and lips on mine.

Love within reach.

By my side.

I desire you in my arms forever.

On the Journey of Being

Your being,
in all of its wishes,
granted.

Working,
accepting,
understand ourselves.

We are one,
rising up in the name of life
and love.

Accepting and punishing ourselves
in all that is unknown.

Moving from illusions and fear.

On a journey
to find yourself the one.

Conquer Mind

You will be presented obstacles.

And you will climb.

And you will fall.

And you will overcome
and fall again.

And as the hills get steeper,
Truth gets deeper,
and you will evolve.

Conquering space.
Conquering thought.

Conquering mind.

Swift Flow/ eternal dance
We are the wind and the air.

The clothes
and hair that blows.

Fascinated by our own.

I am with you.

Dancing the infinite dance.

Around, and through you.

Existing in presence.
In truth and acceptance

Eternally in a swift flow.

Every single thing,
perfection.

All that is touched,
All that is judged.

All that is mistaken.
All decisions made.

As there is only one way.

And chaos does not exist
in the eternal flow of being.

Course of Consciousness/ trial of the galaxies
All you experience is only nature.

A repeating course
for all creatures.

Fighting, dying, multiplying.

Learning, growing.

The grand miracle of existence.

Trial of the galaxies;
All the living must face.

The *course*
of *consciousness*.

Without Free Will
Life is a process.

A course of god.

The fighting,
hate, death,

life and evolution.

Existence and creation.

Completely inevitable.

Without free will.

Course of Mind/ efficient being
Chemicals that make up the brain.

Elements of space.

Takes a course of pain.

Awakening,
thinking.

Choosing
more and more,
the efficient way.

Evolve
Experience is evolution.

To live.
To be.

No matter good, nor bad.

Evolution exists fundamentally.

Striving to understand itself
and live comfortably.

Consciousness;
Consequences.

Eternally awakening by reactions.

Divine Timing/ divinity unfolds
Expressing again.

You find the answer
by struggle and pain.

I write of your arrival.

Patient,
knowing you would show.

Arriving in divine timing.

Children of the Universe
God gives itself a name.

Who are you?

What do you call the young mind?

Ageless;

Children of the universe, playing.

Eternally curious.

Exploring.
Living.

Learning to be itself again.

Fragile
You are fragile.

Divine and still blooming.

Delicately fine tuning.

Not yet meant to be touched
or you will wilt.

And I,
soak in the poisons of your leaf.

Subconsciously/ brain/ programming
Subconsciously,
you are creating.

Subconsciously,
you are practicing,
learning,
perfecting the being

Subconsciously,
information
and concept is forming.

Programming.

Ultimately
I am learning.

I am being.

I am creating.

Surround Yourself/ controlled transformation
Be conscious of patterns that transform you
from one thing to another.

Put your mind in wealth.

Surround yourself
with what you wish to become.

Happiness.

Knowledge.

Creativity
and love.

Or hate,
poison,

and lust.

A Lesson in This Moment/ find the reason this exists
Here,
we meet in lessons of each other.

Be conscious, and grab from me what you can.

Something,
somewhere;

There is truth needed for your collection.

In our words,
our projection and surrounding.

Find the reason this moment exists.

Walking Away/ either way/ inevitable path
It does not matter what happens
from this point on.

The path is the same
for everyone.

Walk away, play life unconscious,
or selfish.

The universe is unbiased.

Save it.

Or forget it.

Either way.

Still on the Path
You are on the path
and there is no way off.

You will arrive in the footprints
of God.

Horrific regrets.

Those hurt.

Each and every accomplishment
and mistake.

All apart.

Still on the path.

War of Mind/ war of the world
There is a war in your mind.

And so a war upon the world.

When it grabs hold,
fighting and anger comes to a release.

And the being come to peace.

Sadness, Rage, and Stubbornness
Cry, its okay.

Things aren't going your way.

And so ready for change.

Rage.
You are bothered.
And with problems to solve.

Be stubborn
and your questions
and skepticism
will be corrected.

Perfect and Passionate Being
To see the beauty.

To become passionate at a glimpse
of truth.

It will change you.

In ignorance,
shake you.

No matter which path is taken.

The perfect and passionate being awakens.

How Creative You Really Are/ creativity
You have built a fantasy.

A character.

A life.

Put meaning and reason
behind each thing.

Built a wall
to defend.

For comfort and favourites

Territory
and competition.

The Creation of God/pleasure and pain
How many times will you touch the stove?

How long will you test me?

Through choices,
slowly wake
with each mistake
and chances you take.

Choosing what,
and what not to experience again.

Over and over,
guilt;

Destruction.

Over and over,
discovery,
pleasures, and pain.

Nothing to Create/ creating falseness
There is no creation,
but in our minds
of what is *not* truth.

Beliefs/ emotions/ blockage
What is believed will be lived.

Anything.

Obscured and distorted.

You will suffer
as mind gets twisted in any order.

There are no rules to belief and emotion.

Only truth and perception.

Be blocked, or know the absolute.

Freed to live in your misconception.

Sickness/ natural selection

You are hurting.

Sick
and dying.

Unable to see the universe,
and so your blood boils
causing disease and reaction.

About to suffer natural selection.

Unable to escape the dangers present
and soon coming.

Overcome the emotion.

Work together as unity.

Come together in harmony.

Set fear aside,
and embrace life.

Escape your rage.

Escape the planet.

Join the galaxy
when you are done
with the animal stage.

Holding onto the Universe/ let go of the universe
Release your views and opinion.

Detach from thought.
and judge none.

Be unblocked
and no longer pained by unknowing.

No longer holding onto the universe.

Perception of Pain/ perception of life
Nothing hurts me.

I am unbelievably in awe.

Blown away.

Impervious to pain.

I know the truth.

No words, nor emotion;

No amount of collision
to my skin and bone
could take my mind off existence.

It is too beautiful for distraction.

No more am I bothered.

Pain, a gift.

And to feel,

beauty.

Perfection.

Reaction/ prisoner of mind
In your fears,
anger and proud moments,

suffer.

Blood rising,
boiling, in the body.

You emotions will guide you.

Stay conscious of triggers

Naturally,
you will create.

In the reactions of
rage, jealousy,
and terror.

Triggers of Mind
I can see reality so fine.

I walk the fine lines.

Morality,
law and emotion.

I will not slip.

I cannot miss.

I understand the triggers,

and desires of mind.

When You're Ready to be Freed/ know the truth
When you are ready to look beyond.

Far, far beyond yourself.

The earth and the stars.

Into the specks of dust.

Into the ultimate infinity.

Deep into the mind.

Turn inward on what is me.

When you are ready to be free,

be freed.

Cured by Knowing/ know the truth
Purity.

Knowing is the cure.

And so healed of disease;

Trauma and anger.

Discomforts.

Healed of hurting.

Hate.

Confusion and mistakes.

Balance and Harmony
There is only Heaven.

Only love,
only god.

I created it.

Molding clouds into the sparks of creation.

Condensed into solid matter of concept.

A pen,
paper and book.

Writing the ways of balance.

Harmony.

One.

We are lovers, loving.
Artists and poets telling stories.

Reciting the picture of existence.

I will show you
how to see and achieve it.

Build, believe, and receive it.

And thus too, be a conscious creator of Heaven.

Waiting patiently
for the world to meet me.

As I express the grand scale of beauty.

The Absolute/ freedom of expression
Live,

in pure acceptance
of self,

and in all that is.

The absolute.

Freedom of expression.

Be free,
and know
that this is God.

Illuminating/ shine on earth
No more hiding.
No more fighting.

Here comes the awakened being;

Shining

Building another new beginning.

Out to set all free.

I give you the truth of everything.

A bright, shining beam;

Illuminating.

Powerful/ magical/ god at work
You are powerful.

A wish granter
in simple words
and action;

Though unrealized and nearly
impossible to communicate.

Tap into your power.

Dip your hand in the jar.

Know who you are.

Take all you want
from the source.

Master
You are the master.

Overcomer of all things.
An inventor and the voice of earth.

Your actions are the truth.

Capable of all imaginable.

Mover of space,
and universe.

Master of mind.

Controlling all that is touched.

Focus
Desire, and fulfillment.

Problem and solving.

Anxiety and breakthrough

Down to detail, focus on the vision.

Now conscious,
grab it when you see it.

Nothing is too good to be true.

Do not hesitate on the number, nor size.

But on the beauty.

It will be delivered
and pulled through.

All You Touch and Speak/ extension of god
Brush with your hands,
truth and gentleness.

Touch everything in reach.

To whom you speak,
plant a seed.

I can do anything.

Actions

Choose wisely of your movement,
your words, disturbances and encounters.

Every action,
a reaction.

Creating in our desires
and dances.

Paying in our ignorance
and projections.

Dance and Sing Your Way into Heaven

Dance and sing your way into heaven.

In the purest form of expression

Your absolute self.

All you want,
all you are.

Wishes,
so be it.

Step by step,
waddle,
hipfully
shake your way in.

Express
Let this be the most important moment of life.

Drop what you are doing.

Create;
Now.

Build and be built.

Express yourself.

Sounds of Being/ choosing to sing.
Those who see,
will sing reality
to set themselves free.

Words, sounds,
songs of being.

And will be sang
so perfectly.

Aloud/ with all of your heart
Undisciplined,
you've gone poor.

Illogical.

Strained, and stressed.

Keeping you sleeping.

Uncontrolled thinking.

Say aloud.

Whatever you want.

Confidently.

Truly.

Singing/ healing
Wailer of pain
and truth.

I have sang the lessons of life.

I have withered away.

My voice gone raw,
and shut.

Healed by my cries.

What Is Created
Disasters and consequences.

Freed to think.
Freed to act.

Freed to put meaning
and create anything.

Enjoy your being.

Its desires.

Everything.

Mirror of Reality/ be created
Lie, and live in lies

Hurt to be hurt.

Kill to be killed.

Create to be created

Love to be loved.

Listen and be heard.

Care and be cared for.

Free and be freed.

Feel and be felt

See, to be seen.

Music/ arts of expression

The universe is calling your name
in every form of expression.

Calling for your attention.

Waving
you down.

Reality are the sounds.

Music fills the air.

Shouting out,
"This is god"

Writer of Reality

Writer of reality.

Hands that hold The Universe.

Create,
or destroy.

Get out your pen.

Write.

The Book is Alive
Reality writes you.

Only waited to be realized.

We are the book.
The pages
and pen.

Already written.

Heaven and Hell/ pit of mind
Imagination
through fear.

Look what we have built here.

Clawing at power and control.

Misinterpretation of
heaven and hell;

By perspective of the books

Each with a different outlook.

Some realized.

Some stuck;

Trapped,
in the pit of mind.

Call and Response/ desire and fulfillment
With each call,
a response.

Granted,
if believed and said.

It will be expressed.

It will be presented.

And you will progress.

What We Say Now/ what we do now
Our dreams are in the words we say.

Actions played.

We can do anything.

Or nothing.

Alone/unheard
Communication is thinning.

I want to be alone.

They are without higher thought.

No deep need to know.

To the world, I am only a noise

Unheard.

So I,
cornered
into solitude.

Seek Silence
When you are mis-
and unheard,
nature will call your name
with all that is not said.

In need of break
from the voices in your head.

Without words.

To process
and be.

In no rush,
nature waits for you.

Ever so patiently.

Sit in Silence
Silently,
I will sit.

You will come to the conclusion of it.

Silence.

The answer falls into my lap.

Saying Nothing
The power of silence.

In all that is not said,

I am created.

Say nothing
at exactly the right time.

Silent Place
In solitude, I can think.

I can hear *me*.

Raged
in noise.

Intolerable to the ignorant voice.

Question who is sane.

Question yourself,
down to dust in space.

The old being
and name.

Shed your skin.

The old way.

Rethinking your beliefs.

Let go
and the answers
will be revealed.

No Reaction
Hold the urge to be bitter
and act.

Sit.

Watch spells play out.

Do not react at all,
as it will question itself
in the gap of silence.

Stumble,
one truth after another.

And arrive at the answer.

Burn Away
Push through the silence.

Put up with your mind.

Burn away what you know.

God wishes to speak.

Listen.

Be tortured by the truth,

Enlightened by discovery.

Stillness
Mankind evolves.

Choosing to only speak the absolute.

Yet not to dwell in the atom,
or existence.

As it is obvious.

No longer confused.

Come to stillness.
Agreed to not speak;

Only breathe.

Without emotion;
Or expression.

Without cries,
and without reaction.

I sit,
alone in silence.

In absolute knowledge.

Man sits in stillness.

Creating God, to live again.

Death to Live Again
Realize life.

Leave the old, behind.

Wake
to what it means to be alive
and living.

I am tingling.
Creating.

My DNA,
dancing.

Death,
transcended by your being.

Obsolete
The world becomes efficient.

Intelligent.

Tools, obsolete.

With no need to work,
sweat or fight for desires.

Becoming comfortable;

And into peace.

Wanting nothing.

Over and Over, Keep Waking/ reborn
Just when I think I am done,
another door opens.

In my mind, there is no possible way
for something deeper.

And I have been wrong
two hundred times or so
in a row.

What You Are Doing/ what you really mean
I see,
and understand your meaningless words.

Troubled reaction.

For deeper reasons
your blood boils.

I feel the pain you are inflicting on me,
and others.

That's okay.

I know what you are doing.

I am conscious of your intentions;

And what you really mean.

Searching for Truth
This is only the beginning.

You will find time.

Patients,
answers along the way.

You will peel back reality
every so slowly,
and be shocked at the beauty of yourself.

Searching for truth.

Searching for you.

Search for Passion/ passion is the universe
What is your attraction?

What do you want more than anything?

Do you desire it enough
to put into action?

Do not settle for less.

Do not take no for an answer.

Do not wait
any longer.

Enjoy, in every way,
your journey of passion.

Follow Your Heart
Be conscious of your heart
calling out.

Know what you want.

So when you see it
cross your path,
it can be grabbed;

Explored and fulfilled.

Around your desires,
the universe is built.

Your changes
and path to achieve.

Enjoy Life Now
Enjoy yourself

The universe is yours.

A playground meant for God.

Play in it.

Be happy.
Be creative.

Leave all behind that does not benefit.

Leave behind what does not make your heart sing.

Stop what you are doing.

And live.

Gentleness
Caress reality with long,
light,
loving strokes.

With a pet
and loving words.

Treat the substance
with kindness.

Gentleness.

Slowly,
softly unfold what is waiting
to be touched.

Unwilling
Those unwilling
never see the big picture.

Existence.
Mind
and reason.

Unwilling to give up
beliefs
that has interpreted reality

Their "Human"

Unwilling to live.

Unwilling to look at itself.

Horrified in their shadow.

Mental Game/ game of physics/ I see the universe
Trial and error.

Over and over,
one thousand times.

The course is set.

Inventions are a domino effect.

All in position.

Pieces aligned.

I see the universe.

I'm ready to play the game.

Make a move and watch everything

fall into place.

Mindset/ patterns
I play with,
and as god.

Myself, in both seats.

I am the board,
players
and pieces.

Every turn and aftermath.

Cause and effect.

I move in reason.

Those Who See/ life comes to me
Those who know
do not speak.

Those who see
transform quickly.

They let it be.

Walk away,
freely.

And all say the same.

"Life comes to me"

Knowers
Knowers
dive head first into life.

Jump in with both feet
and they see the full picture of reality.

Conscious of Creation
Before you create

After you create.

What has been created?

What is done?

Not done?

Become conscious of your creations.

Snap
At the snap of your fingers,
you can create.

At the very thought, desires
are not separate.

Already there.

Effortless.

I am conscious.

All my decision,
delivered.

Entangled Illusion/ my choosing
The world,
everyone in it,
an illusion.

There is nothing;

No one you cannot have.

I choose my dances
with illusion you call your body.

In the illusion you've given a name.

And this illusion we call love.

With what I wish to become;

Entangled.

Illusion of Being
Attached to the illusion,
we are but collections of opinion;

With no truth to be known.

Your clothing.
Impressions.

You are the an illusion of being.

Adopting,
combining matter and personality

Magic of Normality/ book of magic
Born into it,
we are unimpressed
at the magic of normality.

Yet to question
the absolute;

And foresee.

How normal is it,

that we are walking,
talking living things?

Communicating.

Reading
from this book of magic.

Getting the being
to do anything?

Nature Laughs
The wild ride you have been on.

And the expression on your face
the whole way.

Conscious of the concept;

Nature laughs;

As it realizes it is
being controlled.

We are the joke.

Being played upon itself.

Snickering at your waking

Chuckling in your joy.

Laughing,
at all that has gone unnoticed.

Thus far.

Higher and Higher Consciousness
It will hit you.

Harder and harder,
who you are.

Higher and higher,
consciousness continues to climb.

It takes some time to fully realize.

Who,
and what
all this really is.

Species/ temperature/ shapes of being
Precession,

evaporation,

temperature,
vibration
creates the environment;

And so the species.

Rising,
falling
in the light, and shadow.

Heated and cooled.

Printed in shapes
in which consciousness can be carried.

Infinite Fractal Being
Heat upon heat
in the infinite layers of being.

Brain in brain,
neuron in neuron.

Connected.

Infinity in,
infinity out.

Mind

God.

Part of the Great Reality/ piece of the universe/ infinite galaxies
You exist
as part of the big picture.

One of the many gods that walk the earth,
and roam the universe.

Whom are all part of the being.

Only a speck of the great reality.

Drops in drops.

Dots on dots,
packed into the seed we call existence.

Pieces of the infinite galaxies.

Simple Existence, Complex Mind
The world,
reality,
existence is simple.

Though we choose to create.

In our minds, and in actions,
we have created something so complex
out of nearly nothing.

The Universe Is A Seed/ the infinite unfolding
The universe is a brain.

That called "You"
and "me"

Compacted into a seed,
forever unfolding
 into the intelligent being.

Overlooking Heaven
Oceans, rain.
Clouds,
Plants, trees.

Me.
Water, fire, air and earth.

Heaven is here.

Look no further.

The One,
walking in its soil
on two feet.

In smiles,
it reads.

Becomes conscious of its own
blooming.

Perception of the Phenomenon

There is no truth in the universe
but the realization of existence.

And the decision to speak it.

There is nothing,
but the rise and fall of matter.

And perception of the phenomenon.

All else, an illusion.

Matter, motion.

Mind.

And with this simple beauty,
we have created more.

The desire to be loved
and understood.

And the pain of not.

The name.

And the belief of ourselves.

Induction and Capacitance/ acceleration/ magnetism
What is absorbed,
is the induction of radiation.

Capacitance and
acceleration of all things.

Physics of the galaxy.

Sacred geometry.

Discharge and Resistance/ repulsion/ radiation
Discharge is the radiation

Atom to atom,
transferring heat.

What is pushed out, repulsion.

Held up by resistance
to what is released.

Over throwing the maximum capacity.

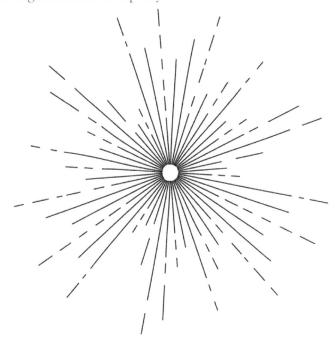

Chapter 3: Nature

Fundamental Existence/ for mind to interpret
Water
Earth
Fire
Air

Space.

It does not matter
what you choose to call it, creator.

Without name.

Physical existence.

And for the mind to interpret.

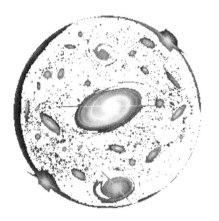

Sky/air/ everything
Sky.

The all,
what looks like none.

Specks of metals, and dusts.

All one.

That
which is put in our lungs.

In which we become,

everything.

Clouds and Lightening/ accumulation/ creation of space
Rising and falling through the earth
and universe.

Condensing,
accumulating particles of the all.

Clashing in static and compression.

Firing at itself,
creating space.

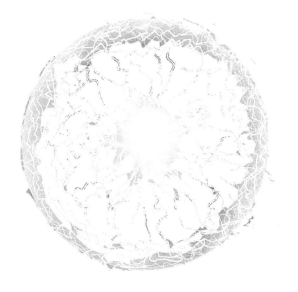

The Art of Reality/ universal pattern
Master the art of reality.

Develop the eye to see.

Find the universal pattern
in everything.

The double helix.

The rise and fall
of the universe

Frequency of Self/ DNA/ matter

All you see,
and all you don't
are the delicate,
extreme frequencies
of the mighty being.

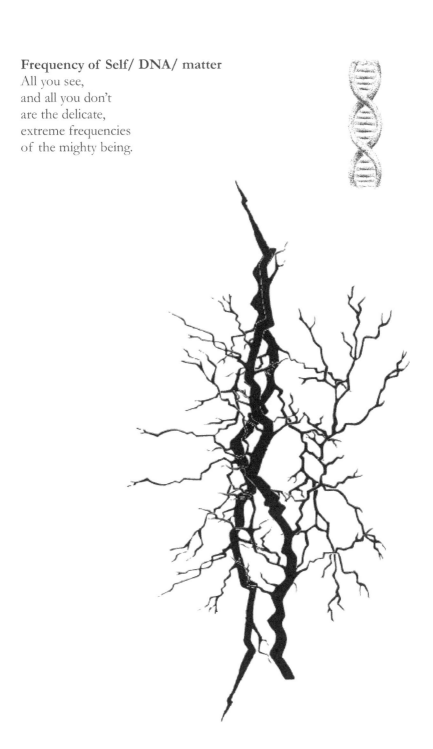

Heat/ radiation
In the warmest,
coolest things.

Rising and falling

Radiating frequency.

Big or small.

In all shapes.

Is the all

Cold/ Ice/ lesser heat/ snow
Temperature comes and goes.

You call it cold;

Ice or snow.

A speck of dust
reaching out
taking shape
of the fractal frequency.

Star/ sun/ core/ molten lava
Look,
deep into the galaxy.

Deeper
into the core of earth.

Find a star.

Sun in the sun.

Surrounding one another.

Seeds of Infinity/ ocean of iron/ accumulation of hydrogen
Seeds of infinity
move like water.

An ocean of iron.

The eternal,
infinite cosmos,

compressing
stars within stars.

Welding metals

in the spiraling
flow of motion.

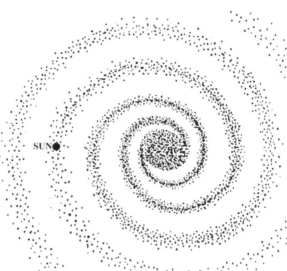

**Oxidizing Iron/ rusted earth/ iron and ice/ corrosion
/chemical weathering**
On this ball of everything,
we call Earth;

Iron.
Ice

Stored away
and released.

Rust.

Chemical reaction
pushing outward
all frequencies of being.

crust
volcano
ash
carbon
plant

Pure potential
of the all.

Mountains/ hill/ texture
Texture on the orb
are the craters,
cracks,
eruptions.

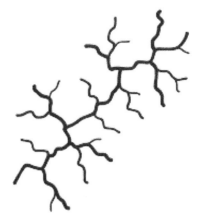

Escaping heat from the core,
rising to the surface

Hills of rock and dirt.

Volcanic Eruption/ smoke/ soot/ rain
Spouting seed of the inner all.

Molten lava
makes it way
through a tunnel.

Soot is laid,
layered.

And smoke gathers water,
raining upon the planet;

Nurturing all released from the vein.

And the world,
self efficient.

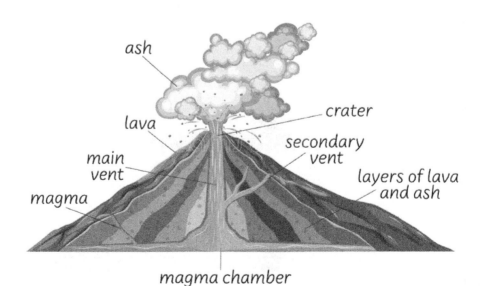

Dirt/soil/ germination

Every blade of grass,
standing tree
and flower;

Mixed into the soil.

Compost,
recycling in the crust.

Balanced upright.

Capacitance, radiation,
breaking through shell
in an up,
down spiral.

South of the seed,
stumped by dirt.

And the north
extended in fractals,
as air is less resistant.

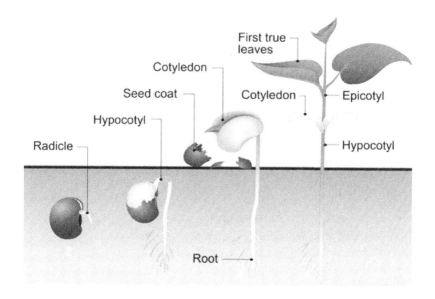

Stem/ tube/ vein/ shoots and roots

Water absorbed, inducted into the seed.
Acting as a straw in the up and down flow
of evaporation, a shoot, root, tube
expanding
the vein.

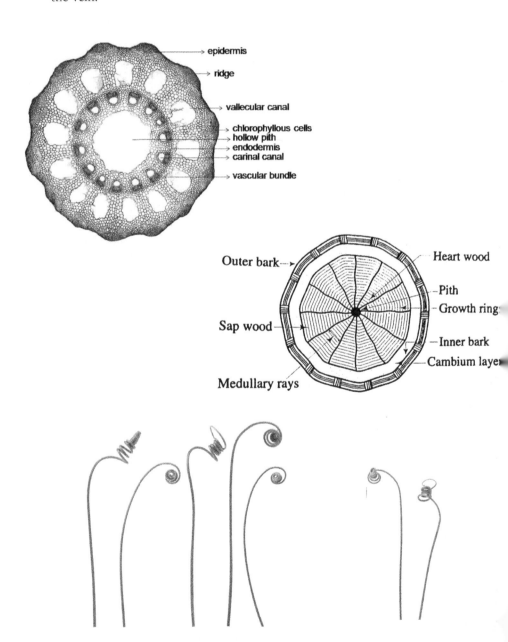

epidermis

ridge

vallecular canal

chlorophyllous cells
hollow pith
endodermis
carinal canal

vascular bundle

Outer bark

Heart wood

Pith

Growth ring

Sap wood

Inner bark

Cambium layer

Medullary rays

Trees
Picture me
as static;

Unfolding.

Trees,
very slow lightening.

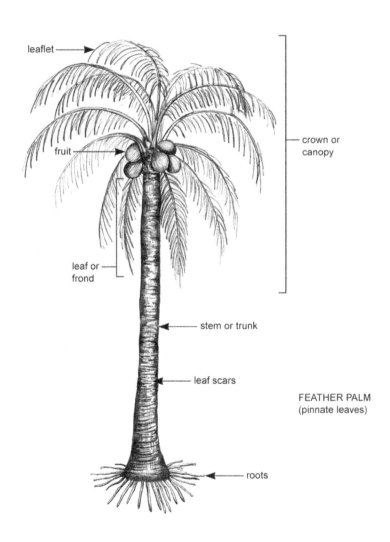

FEATHER PALM
(pinnate leaves)

Leaves/ into the leaf/ fractal vibration
Look
into the fractal vibration of infinity.

The tree itself, a leaf.
Each branch, the tree.
And in all the veins,
a fractal of itself.

fr

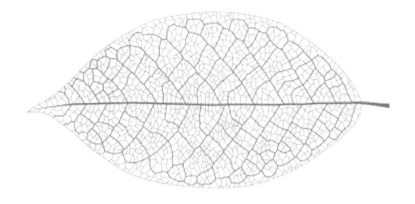

Root System

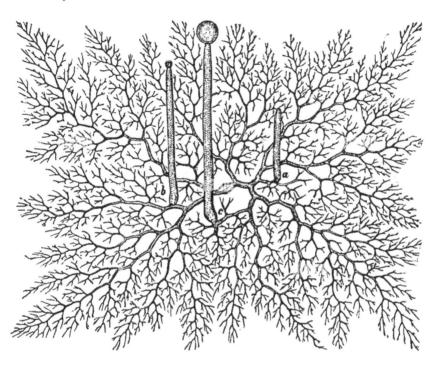

Shapes of God/ vegetables
Spines,
leveled and balance
like a stick in the mud.
Odd shapes
trying to become the sun.

Fingers, roots and limbs
in the resistance
of matter.

The seed falls
and unfolds.

Radiates,
into the many,
and similar shapes
of god.

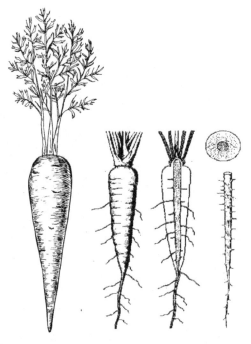

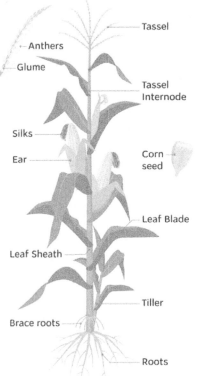

Tassel

Anthers

Glume

Tassel
Internode

Silks

Ear

Corn
seed

Leaf Blade

Leaf Sheath

Tiller

Brace roots

Roots

Nuts and Seeds
Duplications of the star.

Of the brain.

Natures nurturing ways.

In protein.

Milk, children.

The egg.

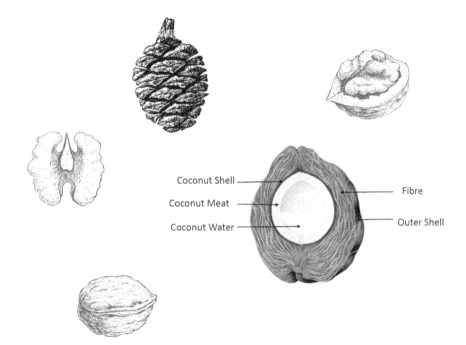

Coconut Shell

Coconut Meat

Coconut Water

Fibre

Outer Shell

Fruit of the Universe

See the stars;

Potential.

Magnetic field pattern.

Blooming,
there is no end.

Infinity is the earth.

Infinity we are.

And forever will be,
fruit of the universe,
takes shape of the all.

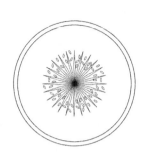

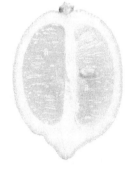

Flowers

At the tip of my root,
I take shape
of the snowflake.

Radiate
out in pedals.

I am the sun
tied to soil.

Efficiency / watering itself
Nature is efficient.

Spread,
curved leaves into funnel
to feed the stem.

Warming,
and watering itself.

Ocean
Balanced, is the water

Resting is the universe.

In a tame vibration.

And the planets, stars and moon,
are the winds,
fighting for its beauty.

Pushing, pulling,
tugging up and down
on the oceans waves.

Sea Floor/ sea creatures

Find creatures
in the shape of the sun.

On the sea floor,
veins and brains in coral.

Swirling tails
and sea shells,
in the shape of the falling universe.

Patterns of lightening.

Beings of the galaxy.

In fractals
floating through space.

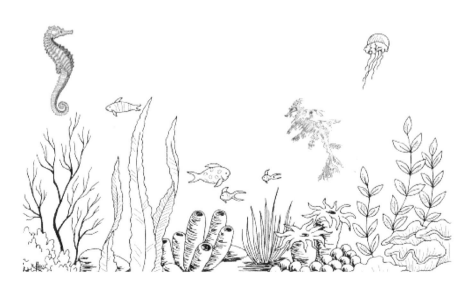

Enchanted Forest/ beauty of nature

Enchanted,
is the existence around you.

Humidity in the air,
and steam fills my lungs.

Animals run,
soar, swim
through the atoms.

I find myself, always,
in the mystical forest that is life.

In it's luscious shapes and colour.

I will walk you through.

Introduce you;

To beauty

Trying to Become Conscious / all the unliving

In law of the universe,

patterns comes to life.

It builds itself.

Everything
trying to become conscious.

Suit of Armor/ body
Tissue and bone.

Muscle, skin and skull.

Overthrown by clothes.

Body in survival.

Heart and brain
with veins,
builds a suit of armor.

Protected
by the harsh substance
that is

reality.

Cerebrum

Brain

Brainstem { Midbrain
Pons
Medulla

Cerebellum

Spinal cord

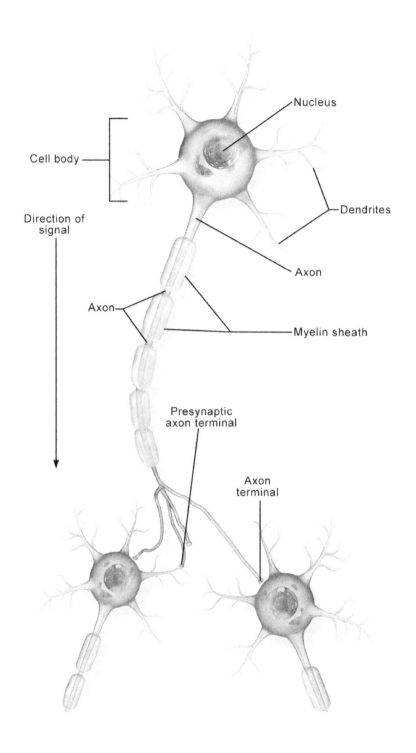

Nucleus

Cell body

Dendrites

Direction of
signal

Axon

Axon

Myelin sheath

Presynaptic
axon terminal

Axon
terminal

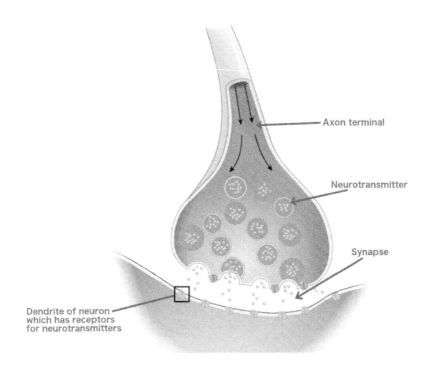

Axon terminal

Neurotransmitter

Synapse

Dendrite of neuron
which has receptors
for neurotransmitters

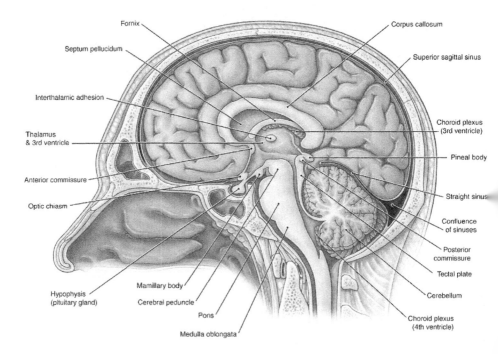

Fornix

Septum pellucidum

Interthalamic adhesion

Thalamus
& 3rd ventricle

Anterior commissure

Optic chiasm

Corpus callosum

Superior sagittal sinus

Choroid plexus
(3rd ventricle)

Pineal body

Straight sinus

Confluence
of sinuses

Posterior
commissure

Tectal plate

Cerebellum

Choroid plexus
(4th ventricle)

Hypophysis
(pituitary gland)

Mamillary body

Cerebral peduncle

Pons

Medulla oblongata

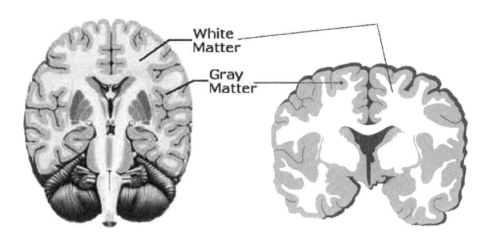

White Matter

Gray Matter

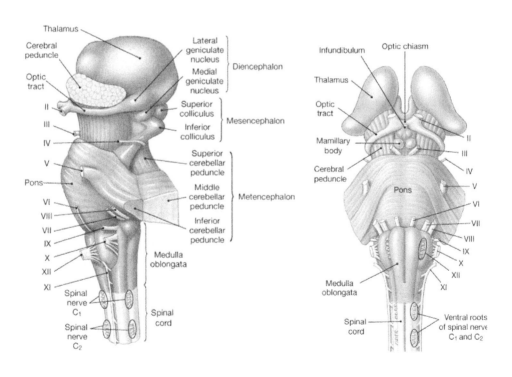

Thalamus

Cerebral peduncle

Optic tract

II

III

IV

V

Pons

VI

VIII

VII

IX

X

XII

XI

Spinal nerve C₁

Spinal nerve C₂

Lateral geniculate nucleus

Medial geniculate nucleus

} Diencephalon

Superior colliculus

Inferior colliculus

} Mesencephalon

Superior cerebellar peduncle

Middle cerebellar peduncle

Inferior cerebellar peduncle

} Metencephalon

Medulla oblongata

Spinal cord

Infundibulum

Optic chiasm

Thalamus

Optic tract

Mamillary body

Cerebral peduncle

Pons

II

III

IV

V

VI

VII

VIII

IX

X

XII

XI

Medulla oblongata

Spinal cord

Ventral roots of spinal nerve C₁ and C₂

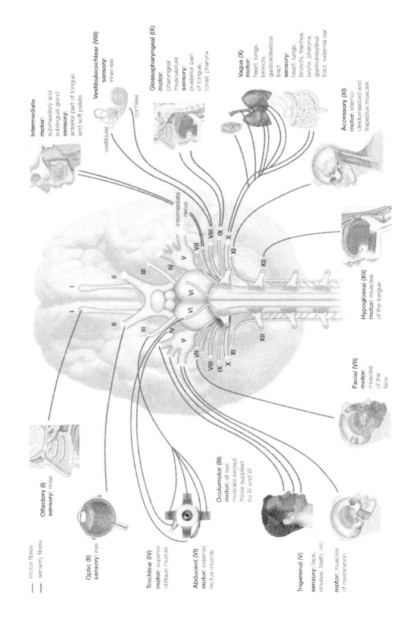

— motor fibres
— sensory fibres

Olfactory (I)
sensory: nose

Optic (II)
sensory: eye

Trochlear (IV)
motor: superior oblique muscle

Abducent (VI)
motor: external rectus muscle

Oculomotor (III)
motor: all eye muscles except those supplied by IV and VI

Trigeminal (V)
sensory: face, sinuses, teeth, etc.
motor: muscles of mastication

Facial (VII)
motor: muscles of the face

Intermediate
motor: submaxillary and sublingual gland
sensory: anterior part of tongue and soft palate

Vestibulocochlear (VIII)
sensory: inner ear

vestibular
cochlear

Glossopharyngeal (IX)
motor: pharyngeal musculature
sensory: posterior part of tongue, tonsil, pharynx

intermediate nerve

Vagus (X)
motor: heart, lungs, bronchi, gastrointestinal tract
sensory: heart, lungs, bronchi, trachea, larynx, pharynx, gastrointestinal tract, external ear

Accessory (XI)
motor: sterno-cleidomastoid and trapezius muscles

Hypoglossal (XII)
motor: muscles of the tongue

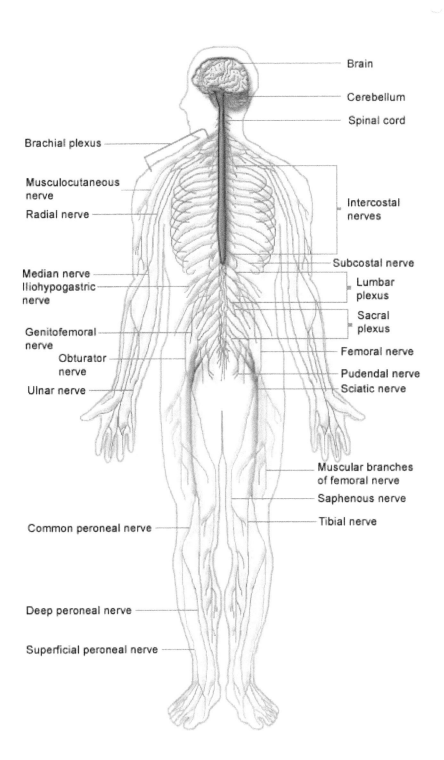

Brain

Cerebellum

Spinal cord

Brachial plexus

Musculocutaneous nerve

Radial nerve

Intercostal nerves

Median nerve

Iliohypogastric nerve

Subcostal nerve

Lumbar plexus

Sacral plexus

Genitofemoral nerve

Obturator nerve

Femoral nerve

Pudendal nerve

Sciatic nerve

Ulnar nerve

Muscular branches of femoral nerve

Saphenous nerve

Common peroneal nerve

Tibial nerve

Deep peroneal nerve

Superficial peroneal nerve

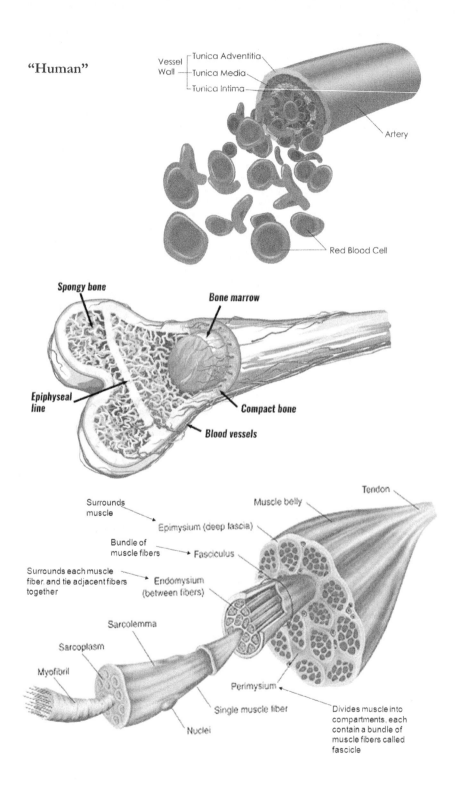

"Human"

Vessel Wall
├ Tunica Adventitia
├ Tunica Media
└ Tunica Intima

Artery

Red Blood Cell

Spongy bone

Bone marrow

Epiphyseal line

Compact bone

Blood vessels

Surrounds muscle → Epimysium (deep fascia)

Muscle belly

Tendon

Bundle of muscle fibers → Fasciculus

Surrounds each muscle fiber, and tie adjacent fibers together → Endomysium (between fibers)

Sarcolemma

Sarcoplasm

Myofibril

Perimysium

Single muscle fiber

Nuclei

Divides muscle into compartments, each contain a bundle of muscle fibers called fascicle

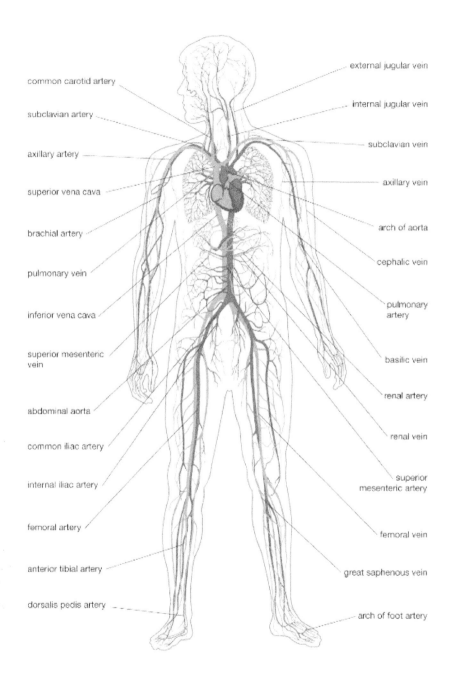

common carotid artery

subclavian artery

axillary artery

superior vena cava

brachial artery

pulmonary vein

inferior vena cava

superior mesenteric
vein

abdominal aorta

common iliac artery

internal iliac artery

femoral artery

anterior tibial artery

dorsalis pedis artery

external jugular vein

internal jugular vein

subclavian vein

axillary vein

arch of aorta

cephalic vein

pulmonary
artery

basilic vein

renal artery

renal vein

superior
mesenteric artery

femoral vein

great saphenous vein

arch of foot artery

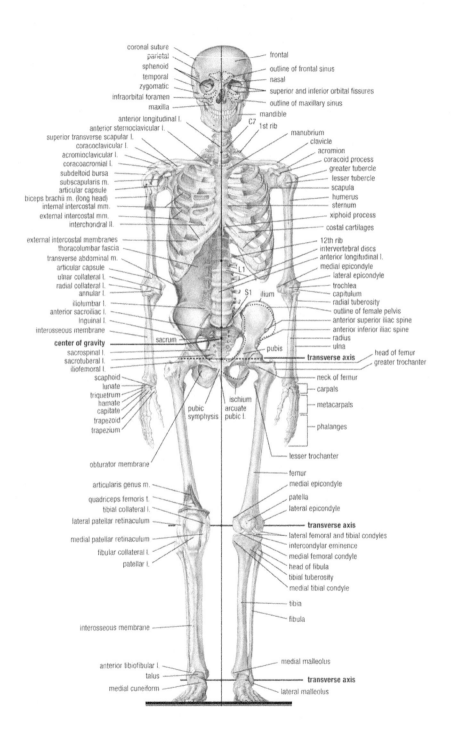

coronal suture
parietal
sphenoid
temporal
zygomatic
infraorbital foramen
maxilla
anterior longitudinal l.
anterior sternoclavicular l.
superior transverse scapular l.
coracoclavicular l.
acromioclavicular l.
coracoacromial l.
subdeltoid bursa
subscapularis m.
articular capsule
biceps brachii m. (long head)
internal intercostal mm.
external intercostal mm.
interchondral ll.
external intercostal membranes
thoracolumbar fascia
transverse abdominal m.
articular capsule
ulnar collateral l.
radial collateral l.
annular l.
iliolumbar l.
anterior sacroiliac l.
inguinal l.
interosseous membrane
center of gravity
sacrospinal l.
sacrotuberal l.
iliofemoral l.
scaphoid
lunate
triquetrum
hamate
capitate
trapezoid
trapezium

obturator membrane

articularis genus m.
quadriceps femoris t.
tibial collateral l.
lateral patellar retinaculum
medial patellar retinaculum
fibular collateral l.
patellar l.

interosseous membrane

anterior tibiofibular l.
talus
medial cuneiform

frontal
outline of frontal sinus
nasal
superior and inferior orbital fissures
outline of maxillary sinus
mandible
1st rib
manubrium
clavicle
acromion
coracoid process
greater tubercle
lesser tubercle
scapula
humerus
sternum
xiphoid process
costal cartilages
12th rib
intervertebral discs
anterior longitudinal l.
medial epicondyle
lateral epicondyle
trochlea
capitulum
radial tuberosity
outline of female pelvis
anterior superior iliac spine
anterior inferior iliac spine
radius
ulna
head of femur
greater trochanter
neck of femur
carpals
metacarpals
phalanges
lesser trochanter
femur
medial epicondyle
patella
lateral epicondyle
transverse axis
lateral femoral and tibial condyles
intercondylar eminence
medial femoral condyle
head of fibula
tibial tuberosity
medial tibial condyle
tibia
fibula
medial malleolus
lateral malleolus

C7
L1
S1
ilium
sacrum
pubis
transverse axis
ischium
pubic symphysis
arcuate pubic l.

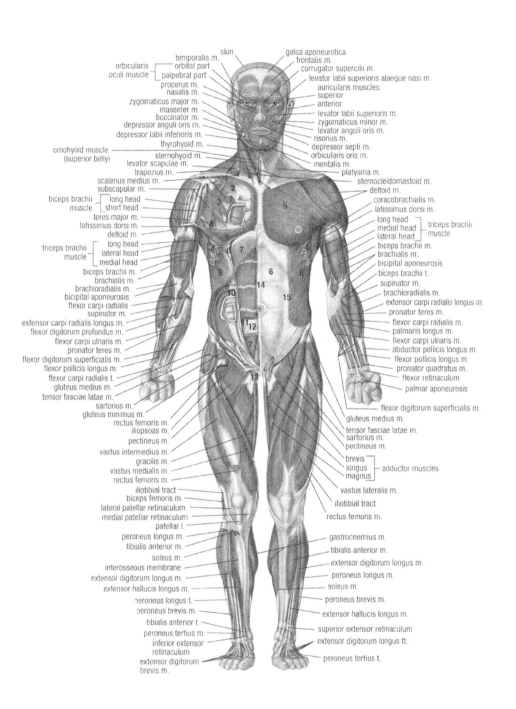

skin
temporalis m.
galea aponeurotica
frontalis m.
orbicularis — orbital part
oculi muscle — palpebral part
corrugator supercilii m.
levator labii superioris alaeque nasi m.
procerus m.
nasalis m.
auricularis muscles:
superior
anterior
zygomaticus major m.
masseter m.
buccinator m.
levator labii superioris m.
zygomaticus minor m.
levator anguli oris m.
depressor anguli oris m.
depressor labii inferioris m.
risorius m.
thyrohyoid m.
depressor septi m.
omohyoid muscle
(superior belly)
sternohyoid m.
levator scapulae m.
orbicularis oris m.
mentalis m.
trapezius m.
platysma m.
scalenus medius m.
sternocleidomastoid m.
subscapular m.
deltoid m.
biceps brachii — long head
muscle — short head
coracobrachialis m.
latissimus dorsi m.
teres major m.
latissimus dorsi m.
deltoid m.
long head
medial head — triceps brachii
lateral head — muscle
triceps brachii — long head
muscle — lateral head
medial head
biceps brachii m.
brachialis m.
bicipital aponeurosis
biceps brachii t.
biceps brachii m.
brachialis m.
brachioradialis m.
bicipital aponeurosis
flexor carpi radialis
supinator m.
supinator m.
brachioradialis m.
extensor carpi radialis longus m.
pronator teres m.
extensor carpi radialis longus m.
flexor digitorum profundus m.
flexor carpi ulnaris m.
pronator teres m.
flexor digitorum superficialis m.
flexor pollicis longus m.
flexor carpi radialis t.
gluteus medius m.
tensor fasciae latae m.
flexor carpi radialis m.
palmaris longus m.
flexor carpi ulnaris m.
abductor pollicis longus m.
flexor pollicis longus m.
pronator quadratus m.
flexor retinaculum
palmar aponeurosis
sartorius m.
gluteus minimus m.
rectus femoris m.
iliopsoas m.
pectineus m.
flexor digitorum superficialis m.
gluteus medius m.
tensor fasciae latae m.
sartorius m.
pectineus m.
vastus intermedius m.
gracilis m.
vastus medialis m.
rectus femoris m.
brevis
longus — adductor muscles
magnus
iliotibial tract
biceps femoris m.
lateral patellar retinaculum
medial patellar retinaculum
patellar l.
vastus lateralis m.
iliotibial tract
rectus femoris m.
peroneus longus m.
tibialis anterior m.
soleus m.
interosseous membrane
extensor digitorum longus m.
extensor hallucis longus m.
gastrocnemius m.
tibialis anterior m.
extensor digitorum longus m.
peroneus longus m.
soleus m.
peroneus longus t.
peroneus brevis m.
tibialis anterior t.
peroneus tertius m.
inferior extensor
retinaculum
extensor digitorum
brevis m.
peroneus brevis m.
extensor hallucis longus m.
superior extensor retinaculum
extensor digitorum longus tt.
peroneus tertius t.

Skin/ touch
Skin.

My body is an efficient receiver
picking up signal.

I am a conductor.

Nerves of vibration.

Through touch,
I avoid pain
in order to survive.

Gravitate to that which brings pleasure.

Sensations, throughout my body.

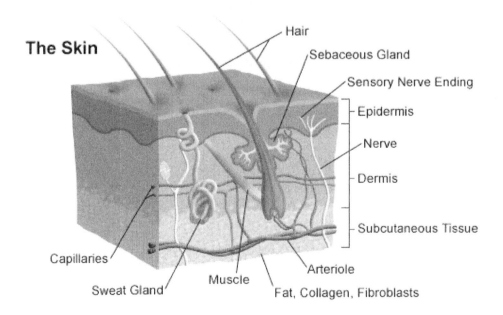

The Skin

Hair
Sebaceous Gland
Sensory Nerve Ending
Epidermis
Nerve
Dermis
Subcutaneous Tissue
Capillaries
Arteriole
Sweat Gland
Muscle
Fat, Collagen, Fibroblasts

Hair

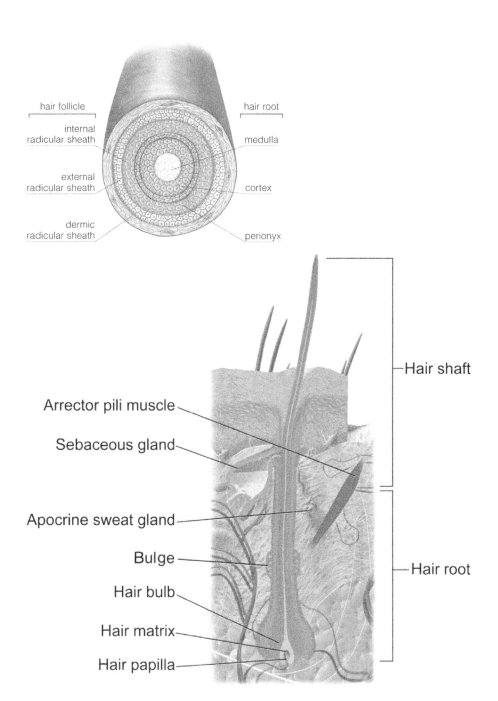

hair follicle

internal radicular sheath

external radicular sheath

dermic radicular sheath

hair root

medulla

cortex

perionyx

Arrector pili muscle

Sebaceous gland

Apocrine sweat gland

Bulge

Hair bulb

Hair matrix

Hair papilla

Hair shaft

Hair root

Hearing/ ears

I hear the matter.
I am alert.

There is a difference in vibrations of tone.

Listening for screams;
or poetry.

Cries
touching the thin skin
of my ear drum,
and I come,
or go
running.

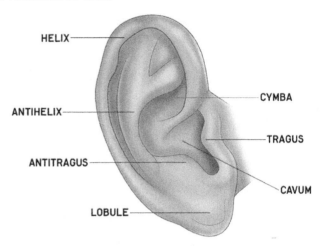

HELIX

CYMBA

ANTIHELIX

TRAGUS

ANTITRAGUS

CAVUM

LOBULE

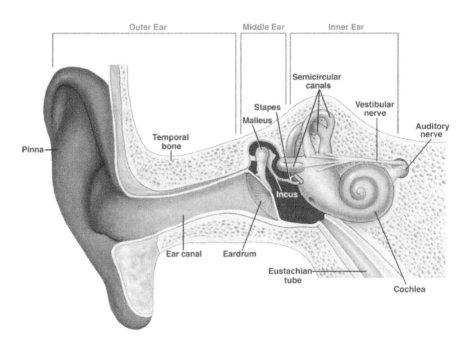

Outer Ear   Middle Ear   Inner Ear

Semicircular
canals

Stapes
Malleus

Vestibular
nerve

Temporal
bone

Auditory
nerve

Pinna

Incus

Ear canal   Eardrum

Eustachian
tube

Cochlea

Smell/ senses

There is a smell in the air.

Rotting, or fresh.

Something to
consume,
or death.

And my senses
guide me.

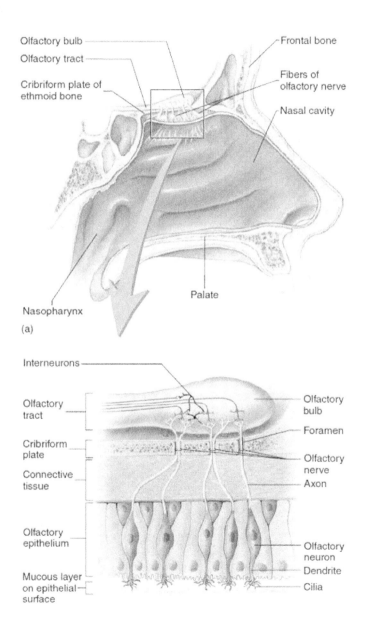

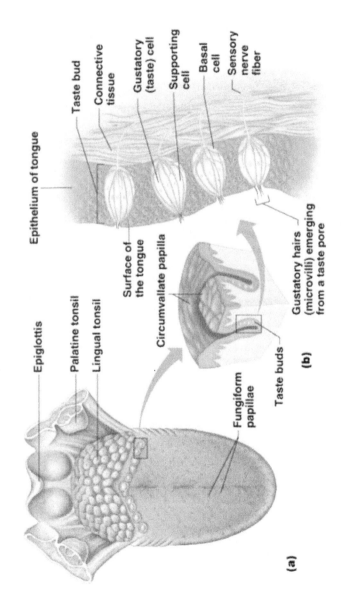

Epiglottis

Palatine tonsil

Lingual tonsil

Fungiform papillae

Taste buds

Circumvallate papilla

Surface of the tongue

Epithelium of tongue

Taste bud

Connective tissue

Gustatory (taste) cell

Supporting cell

Basal cell

Sensory nerve fiber

Gustatory hairs (microvilli) emerging from a taste pore

(a)

(b)

Sight
You are fundamental.

The eye.

The conscious being
Observing everything.

Look around,
at the heaven created
by all
that is law.

I see you.
Reflecting back.

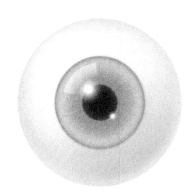

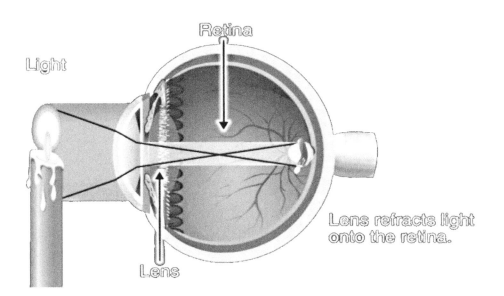

Light

Retina

Lens

Lens refracts light onto the retina.

Reproductive Organ

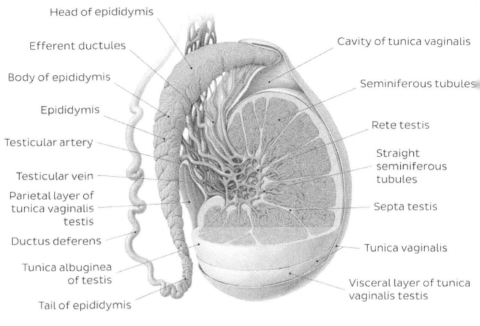

Head of epididymis

Efferent ductules

Body of epididymis

Epididymis

Testicular artery

Testicular vein

Parietal layer of
tunica vaginalis
testis

Ductus deferens

Tunica albuginea
of testis

Tail of epididymis

Cavity of tunica vaginalis

Seminiferous tubules

Rete testis

Straight
seminiferous
tubules

Septa testis

Tunica vaginalis

Visceral layer of tunica
vaginalis testis

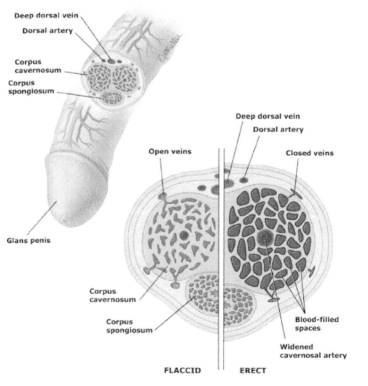

Deep dorsal vein

Dorsal artery

Corpus
cavernosum

Corpus
spongiosum

Glans penis

Deep dorsal vein

Dorsal artery

Open veins

Closed veins

Corpus
cavernosum

Corpus
spongiosum

Blood-filled
spaces

Widened
cavernosal artery

FLACCID   ERECT

Find the Universe in Me/ the great all
I contain earth,
the stars,
the infinite.

Mechanics of the great all.

Find the universe

in me.

Layered in perfect chemistry.

Heartbeat/ born
We are the pulsing fire.

The electric shock,

deep within the universe,

Waiting
to be born.

The heart beat.

Vibrating through the being.

Earth,
living.

Breathing.

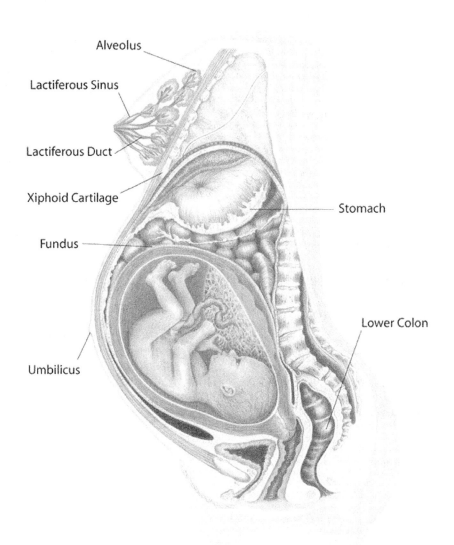

Alveolus

Lactiferous Sinus

Lactiferous Duct

Xiphoid Cartilage

Fundus

Umbilicus

Stomach

Lower Colon

Chapter 4: Creator

Testing the Waters
I have picked it apart.

Rebuilt the universe.

Atom by atom.

It is all God
and without mistake,

it is me.

All decision and thought.

Everything.

If I can think it,
I can build it.

I must test the waters;

As creator.

Play/ work
I have spelled myself;

Again with the wrong song.

So I have much *playing* to do.

Books to write.

Sculpts to sculpt.

A canvas to paint.

Minds to build.

A world to create

I Will Create the World
There is a shift in reality

as ink leaves my pen.

Soaking through the paper.

Coming true, before dying.

I can't stop writing.

Life and existence inspires me.

I will create the world,
using only poetry.

Create Reality
I create reality.

I shift all that around me.

No matter the odds.

Reaching out.

Grasping firmly,

anything.

Create in Pain/ create in love
Today I write in wishes.

Desire and sadness;

That you are not
yet in my arms.

But in joy,
and excitement,
knowing you will be;

Created.

Sculpture/ sculpting

A block of marble.

I will sculpt.

Create all ever hoped.

A masterpiece.

I am conscious
of the corners, and edges.

I am conscious;
of the stone.

The tool, and my surroundings.

The air I breath.

I hold in deeply,
a breath to release.

And in one swing,
the sculpt is complete.

Coming to life;

Chiseled and polished;

A new door.
Carved,
for you.

Walk through.

The Shape of You
I feel the chills,
still underneath your nails.

Lip marks
that never left.

Teeth,
imprinted on my neck.

I will draw your body.

Shadow you in, once again
with freckles.

Each to be kissed.

Forever remembrance
of how you taste.

It is so clear.

So very real.

Like you are here.

Still
Right next to me.

Reality,
in the shape of you.

Blank Canvas
Be inspired by the blank canvas.

Knowing there is much room to create.

Space for imagination
and nothing is yet known.

Trust in your tools.

Examine the bristles.

Carefully question
your colours and brush.

Now paint;

And do not hesitate
in your strokes.

Painting/ infinite fractal pattern
Lay down a background
so you can see the all.

The deepest purple.
And pokes of stars.

I will paint the universe.

Earths, upon earths.

Each, inside the other.

Blues and reds distant dots.

Sprinkled stars of silvers.

Layered;

Rainbowed by temperature.

Air, water, earth. Fire.

A spinning center
in an infinite, fractal pattern.

Write Poetry/ oh, what heaven
Find the hidden answers.

Down to their details,
in the meaning of each word,

you will draw back to god.

Down to this very moment.

It is heard.

Enjoy your freedom.

To write poetry for life.

Oh,
what heaven.

Specifically
Write out every heart beat
shared.

The line of foot prints
left in the sand.

Every breathe and touch of hand

ss it will come true.

Created,
loved,
and understood by you.

Down To Her Last Freckle/ I will sing your name
Reality is created in your image.

Deep in the details.

Down to your deepest desires.

Say wealth,
say love.

Received in your poetry.

It will come.

So give me beauty

One to please.

One who speaks to me in poetry.

The One I Love

Life is a stage.

I wail in pain.

"Lover;

Singer;

Passionate being.

One I love.

Love me
for me."

Coming
I feel it coming in the breath of my lungs.

My pulsing heart.

Tingling in my being;

You are listening.

Eyes closed,
Walk in trust.

Heaven is known when you're ready.

I will see you soon.

Every breath brings you near me you.

Victory of the People/ who is like god
He,
who is like God;

And she,
victory of the people.

It is written
in the name.

And in the stars,
to rise atop,
another war is won.

Our right,
our time,
and destiny.

Our place to create.

Our time to free
and be freed.

Fall in Love
Today,
I sit with a notebook
under a tree.

I see so much beauty.

Being with you,
is my heaven.

And I would wait,
and write for an eternity.

I would stare deeply
into the mind of us.

The universe.

With my pen and paper;
I would sit still;

Listen, and put in poem
the most romantic poem ever told.

Falling in love.

Technology Witch/ cosmic wizard/ the truth of existence
Thought alone.

Their mind moves reality.

Witches and wizards;

Gazing into a world of insanity.

Into future,
into past.

Bringing forth inventions,
knowledge and wisdom.

Technology.

Cosmic understanding.

Communicating

the truth of existence.

Illusion Dancer
She knows herself, god.

Unbiased,
dancing *with* the illusion.

Without assumption.

Balanced;

Expresses poetically.

Dancing with me.

I Know You Exist
I see that only my dreams come true.

I know you exist.

I created you.

Finally,
I can rest,

knowing the truth of this.

Meet Me in the Sand

Sand and waves.

Lips
to be kissed.

In this
torturous humidity.

Foam at my feet.

Sweat dripping
into the salt sea.

Waiting.

Down by the Water/ waiting
Waiting for us.

Reality
to be created;

She's there,
waiting for me.

In her mind
and in mine.

Waiting to be held,
A hand.

Waiting
in the water and sand.

A kiss,
waiting to be had.

Love,
to be met.

A Written Reality
Strolling through sunshine.

Soon, mine.

Awaiting a kiss
down by the shoreline.

So soon to hold hands.

Word for word
exactly as planned.

Reality
written in the sand.

On my way to you, love.

Blue Eyed Heaven
Beauty.

Look deep into me.

The sand and water match your eyes.

I see the ocean and skies.

I hear waves and wind.

Touching
my skin.

I find heaven in you.

Dust of the universe

Looking back
in awe,

that we are that.

Wholeheartedly in love.

In the Light, in The Shadow
Dancing in the light.

Romantic in the shadow.

Move
with me
under the sun.

And kiss me
under the moon

And the waves,
and stars be our witness.

Innate Pulse
We are the water
and iron.

Heart and blood.

The jolting electricity in our veins.

Dance with me.

With love,
let us move all things

As know,
that this is god.

Garden Bed

I've made a bed.

Drawn in ink with my pen;

Roses, wildflower and blueberry.

I've grown
through winter, and spring.

Beautiful,
and delicious things.

It is us, I am drawing.

Thinking.

Imagining our time in the garden
of being.

Envisioning
soft soil
taking shape of your spine.

And me

taking you,
completely.

Blossom Tree
Run through a pink forest.

In our dreams
and in reality.

For all eternity;

Timelessly,

love me,

live,
surrounded by a garden of blossom trees.

Speak life into me
with poetry.

Whispers of Passion
All so passionately whispered;

Stored in my book.

Shivers,
delivered to my spine.

Out through my skin.

I remember each one of them.

Ever lasting words
of truth
and wisdom.

Breathing through out my body.

Making Love and Poetry
Whisper to me,
words of the absolute.

Melt me in gentleness.

Kiss me with a soft touch.

Say you want more.

Tell me you're in love.

Breathe In Me
Put your body to mine.

Inhale.

Exhale deeply.

Share the air with me.

One kiss so enlightening.

I am fulfilled
just by your breathing.

Princess Castle/ cup runneth over
I will build a castle.

Of any colours she'd choose.

An over sized throne
made of stones.

Precious,
like the princess.

A queen, beside me
up to her neck in the dream.

And a tower high enough to see the world.

Books,
to the ceiling.

And cast spells of peace
to the kingdom.

Writing Back Our Wings/ painted wings
Protecting each
in their fear
and shivering.

Pen to paper,
I write back the hidden power
of the angels.

Drawing,
shading,
and colouring.

Big,
beautiful
feathered wings
that cradle the earth.

Wrapped in warmth.

In beauty
and in awe of themselves.

Save The World
Save the world, my brain screams.

Not necessary, my heart knows.

Enjoy yourself.

That is enough.

We are in no danger.

The angels dance in their desires.

Good or bad,
happy in the lessons learned.

Closing the Book/ it is done
Again,
I find myself in the sun.

Writing about the beauty of one.

Note book swinging,
strolling, singing.

Knowing reality is reality.

My blood tingling;

Knowing it is done.

Closing the book of heaven.

Already,
The world is changing.

Chapter 5: Presence

In and Out
Oh, what pain it is
to be in and out of presence.

What horror and beauty it is
to exist.

In and out;

Moment by moment,
it is misery.

Almost envious for those
who refuse to help themselves.

Never to have touched heaven.

Examine Me Closely
Put me under glass.

Study me.

Pay attention.

Learn my moves.

Examine me closely
and stay conscious
of what,
and all
you are doing.

Beacon
Across the galaxy,
I spotted your light.

Drawn to it, irresistibly.

Your beauty.

Glowing,
shining;

Brighter than the all.

Meet Me, Now
Let us create.

Return to presence.

Meet me.

Now.

Love at First Sight/ I know you are the one
By your smile,
I know you are the one.

In the choice of words said,
and the focus in your eyes on mine.

I *know* you are the one.

.

In the symmetry of your being.

Your stance, and dancing.

Completely balancing.

I *know* you are the one.

Pick Yourself Up/ come back to reality
So many times,
love has laid you down.

Yet, here you are.

Unable to walk away
from the beauty that is.

Pain,
desire;
Belief.

Picking yourself up,

choosing
to live and love again.

Conscious Being
Conscious being.

You are a mirror.

You are reality.

Here to understand the truth of me.

Forever Present/ foreverness
Life.

Ageless,
timeless.

Foreverness.

An eternity.

I am present.

Welcome Home/ step into yourself
Left,
to find yet again,
standing at the door mat.

Welcome home,
and enjoy
what you have.

Your box of toys.
Old drawings,
maps,
inventions and ideas.

Step into yourself.

That,
which has always been.

God Playing in Heaven/ god is heaven
I am in heaven.

Splashing around in sand, and shell.

Sea foam at our ankles;

The water is warm
and the air,
humid.

Ill chase you.
You chase me
and we'll be free.

We'll forget reality.

Live in the moment;

Passionately.

Fully,
truthfully.

Experiencing this being

we call,
Heaven.

Unbelievable
Your appearance is unreal.

Your beauty,
too unbelievable for words.

I can't stop smiling at the magic.

Almost disturbing
how real this actually is.

Is This Correct?/ I must be dreaming
I know.
I see, touch, taste,
hear;

Think the all.

I exist,
and this is god.

Is this correct?

Without Doubt
I can see god in your stride.

In every footstep and word.

Your intentions
and all you've yet to find.

I am madly in love.

And without doubt,
this is god.

I Know God When I See It
Perfect.
Passionate.
Beauty.
I know god when I see it.

What You Have Shown Me
I cannot un-see.

Un-hear,
or un-know.

Not after what you have shown me.

And with our true selves seen,
will enlighten the earth.

We are the stars;

Shining light on reality.

What I Long To Say
I couldn't possibly tell,
or show how much
I love you.

For there are no words.

But I will get there, somehow.

I will spend existence
searching
for that perfect poem
that enlightens you of your beauty.

Dance around it
until then.

My Deepest Expression
Pulling out the old book again.
Breathing life into the pages.

I told myself,
there was no longer need
of expression.

And then you come along.

One to write down.

I've not been so struck.

I Love You
You know what I want and need;

Exactly.

You touch me in ever word
chosen to
and not say.

Take me.

My life.

All that I am.

Be with me.
Free me.

I love you.

Please Love Me
Love me for the rest of living.

Here, now.

I am madly hurting.

In love with
what is happening.

Weeping in God/ magic around us
I weep at the magic,
flowing through us.

We are the magicians,
moving itself.

What is known,
what is revealed and seen.

Rediscovering infinity.

What beauty
between us.

Standing in Potential
Here we stand in agreement.

Pure potential.

We can do anything.

Deep in the dream of you and me.

Where we are creating.

Excited/ pulled by truth/ dancing blood
My heart and blood
jump and heats in your presence.

I am excited.

Tingling.

Static flows
through my body.

I'm free to move.

And in knowledge
or good news,

my innards have my attention.

And I am being pulled
by the understanding of truth.

Knowing
what I am doing
is reality.

Beauty
What magnificence I have been shown.

Lifted.

I wish nothing more than to continue this adventure.

Absolutely in love.

And without goodbye,

I will see you soon,
beauty.

My Angel/ love of my life
She is my angel.

Love of my life.

God.

Everything.

Create With Me
Everything we need.

Music, brushes;
Love.

Heaven;
Right here.

Create with me.

And with our bare hands,
mold reality.

Before You Answer
Deep inside,
your heart answers.

Your body knows the truth.

Before the first letter
leaves your lips;

You have already answered.

By the way you look;

And shine, freely,
in the light of living.

And the decision is made in the instant
the question is asked.

Say Yes/ mind, body, soul
Say yes,
no matter what.

I want crazy.
I want to live.

I want you;

Everything.

Love me now.

Mind, body and soul.

I want it all.

On Your Hand, the Universe Sits/ moving space
I know that I am in Heaven.

I wrote it;

Looking deeply at the meaning
and cause of creation.

I move space.
I am space.

And the effect.

And so now,
I hold the universe in my hands.

And give back
a little piece of me.

Ring/ torus
I have molded with my mind,
the universe;

Into beauty.

Into the shape of a ring
and set you
in the center.

We are tied together.

Experiencing, always,
remembrance of our existence.

To be together;

Never separate.

We were always meant,
and this,
being the only meaning,
and reason for life.

The search of you,
in a game
of eternal hide and seek.

Bonded by soul.

Again,
so madly in love.

Angelic/ angels of the forest
All that exists,
all that is;

This creation,
this thought.

This decision are the cosmos at play.

They are angels of the forest.

These hands,
these eyes.

Realizing themselves;

Angelic.

And the stars pour upon their head.

The Brightest
In a universe made of stars,
you are the brightest.

Shiniest
and most beautiful in the sky.

I want to live by your side.

Over and over,
dry and die.

Forever left to find, and be surprised.

My Star
You are my star in the universe.

You are my world.
My moon.

My life, forever revolves
around you.

Stars In Your Eyes
All I see, are the infinite stars
of beauty.

Your eyes, skin, and freckles;

I see;
Through and through;

The universe.

I live
and love because of you.

I Choose You
I see the absolute.

In every word,
thought and action
you do.

The truth.

In all the world,
I choose you.

Romantic Universe/ you and me
In creation,
love
and ultimately,

romance is what exists.

And so always found.

The universe looks,
and reflects back into the eyes.

Falls in love,
over and over.

Inevitable.

Word for word
In the fundamentals of poetry.

You and me.

In Your Arms
In your arms,
all goes away.

No death,
no pain.

But love.

You, me
This.

Freedom
from thought,
fear and illusion.

Only knowing.

As I rest
in you.

This is Heaven
Don't let our eyes stray away.

Stay.
Do not hesitate.

This is heaven.

Don't ever leave.

Wrap me in your warmth
and don't let go.

No.

This is heaven,
and all to come.

Tears shed
when I'm gone.

All part of the beauty
to find you and create on repeat.

What is desired, fulfilled, bonded.
It is you.

Heaven.

Pain,
life, existence.

The experience of presence.

This is Heaven.

Trust
In her,
trust.

And him,
in return.

Wake me of my mistakes.

Sooth me in my cries.

And trust that we will be reminded
who we are and why.

Knowing
we can never fail;

Never fall.

In the comfort of our trusted arms.

Oh, the Beauty.
You are so beautiful.

From your eyes,
I see me
finding you.

And you, me.

This is living.

I am coming back to body.

Loving every piece.

Reason to Live
I become what I understand.

I have faced love,
and seen myself.

In my heavy breath,
heartbeat
and tears.

Finding reason to live.

All I Could Ask For
I cannot believe what has presented itself.

Dreams,
desires.

Wrapped up in a bow, for me.

Prayers and wishes
all come true.

Absolutely mine,
in the palms of my hand.

All I could ask for.

Waiting to be delivered.

Home
You tickle me.

Every time you speak.

I am glowing.

Held up by your poem.

I feel loved.

I feel *this* is home.

Choosing Love
Fall into the spells of myself.

I am pained,
by loving
and knowing.

Good, bad.

Equal.

I choose the all.

To love
and to live.

Love Song
My heart,
my being
is singing your name.

In perfect tune
and lyrics
that drive you into my arms.

The universe is listening.

The universe comes running.

The Universe Echos Your Name
I second guess what I know.

I've almost let go of hope.

Each time
on my last straw and dime.

Drawn
in a new direction.

Listening, waiting.

Even after waking and waking.

This journey points here.

To you.

In echos of your name.

Listening/ the stage chooses you
The big screen.

Circle of listeners

Wooden platform.

A dirt mound.

No matter what,
you will form a crowd.

And they will listen.

Raise your voice.

Stand.

Speak the truth,
Be it the absolute.

And be heard.

Your poetry.
Your cries
bringing all forth;

Closer.

Voice Box
My heart is in the shape of your song

and I sing with you.

Vibrating;

Loudly in key.

In harmony
with all you are saying.

And am drawn to your calling.

Soft
I hear you.

It is undeniable.

Soft as an angel.

Pure as a child.

With fire,
fit to change the world.

Your voice slide under me.

Moves me.

Wrapped in the warmth
of your demands.

And my body tingles in the hum of your tone.

Struck
I trust that in every move,
and word said, is pure.

And so too,
poetry.

We are the words.

The singer,
song and dance.

The universe
always,
always struck by romance.

Poet of My Awakening
Without the slightest doubt,
I've had it in mind
my whole life.

Exactly this.

Down to the specifics.

You are my dream.

All there has ever been for me.

This caliber of beauty
and beyond.

You are so much more.

Parts of me, I hadn't seen.

And you are the poet of my awakening.

Existence Exists

Can you believe the beauty that is said?

Heaven, life, god, self;

Only perception.

Can you believe it?

Existence exists.

Speechless Poet

In your voice,
a poetic melody.

Your words move me.

Silent me.

In the way you sway;

A poet of motion,

In touch with mind.

I am speechless.

Prison of Expression/ beyond expression
No matter how hard I try,
I cannot express enough.

No amount of poetry,
no words,
no actions
could convey the magnificence.

The heaven
I see in you.

Laughter, Passion and Play
The universe is laughter passion and play.

Eternally,
Children of the stars.

Laughing,
Passionately playing.

Laughing Poets
You makes me laugh.

Your projection is contagious.

The universal sign of peace,
truth
and consciousness.

I am so happy
when your cheeks rise,
and a crinkle forms in your eyes.

And I know when you are laughing at,
and with me.

Living Like Your Last Day
At any moment,
we can set the course.

Destruction.
Creation.

We are god.

To bring heaven,
or torch the world.

I leave it up to you
what we do.

It is in your hands,
and I am only here to be.

Without rush,
we have forever.

Whenever you are ready.

Happy
with whatever you decide.

And until then,
let us live today
like the last day of our lives.

The One Who Fits
We are a puzzle piece.

Meant to be together.

You fit in my arms,
so perfectly.

And I,
in yours.

A Poem For You/ the poem that set all free
You,
in all the world,

all the galaxy,

in all the universe.

The most beautiful
thing in existence.

More
than this brilliant mind could imagine.

More
than these hands and pen could write.

The perfect poem that sets all free.

Heaven.

Adventure In The Stars/ calling my name
I come out to look at the moon.

It reminds me of you.

I hear the adventure of us;
In violin.

When I look up at the stars,
I see the ocean,

And it is you I imagine.

I hear your voice
singing to me.

Twirling
and laughing
so beautifully.

Calling
and calling

so deeply and desperately;

Our names.

Sun and Moon
Stars,
that twinkle
brightest in the night sky.

Each minute that passes by,

endless.

Time with you
is non existent.

The Sun
and the Moon.

Pushing and pulling
forever.

Heat in the air,
rising and falling.

Holding us up.

Illuminating earth into bloom.

And in your warmth,

I've wondered
how I got to be so lucky.

Water, Light, and Shadow/ waves of water
We are waves of water,
clashing.

Dancing in the light
and shadow.

A romantic universe,
kissing earth.

And with our breath,

A breeze,
creating language;

Forever trying to express
the beauty.

On a life mission,
to find ourselves.

Eternal Love
Kiss me,
always in the same awe
of our first.

Hold my hand,
eternally.

Find me,
love me, infinitely.

Return to Earth
The universe;

Spirals,
into life.

Returning to earth;

Sharing life once more
in the waves.

The confusion,
sleep, and pain.

The wait,
and awakening.

It is so worth it.

Just to be here;

With you,
in Heaven.

The Creation of Poetry/ creation of heaven/ illusion of poetry
We are the elements;

Playing the game of existence.

Rediscovering who
and what this is.

We are the planets and stars.

Whispering wind
into each others ear.

Only sound in the air.

Imagining meaning behind our words.

In the illusion
of poetry.

There is Nothing More Beautiful
A forest of bamboo.

Morning dew.

There is nothing more beautiful than you.

As this is all there is.

Nothing
quite like the bits of salt and shell
in harmony of sand.

Nothing.

Nothing more beautiful
than us;

Holding hands.

Nothing
could compare

to the songs of perception
put in the air.

Walking atop of the poem.

In the awareness
of ourselves.

.

Made in the USA
Monee, IL
04 April 2023

31249302R00125